Stephen Quinlan is an avid sports fan. He has taken some of the greatest memories in sports and tries to capture them in small poetic verses. A style that not only resonates with the reader but a style that gives its content a new accessibility.

I dedicate this book to my wife, who held her son as he passed away. This heartbreaking experience inspired me to write a poem. I found this experience to be so cathartic that I decided to write about my experiences and emotions evoked by sporting greatness.

Stephen Quinlan

ICONS

AUSTIN MACAULEY PUBLISHERS™

LONDON • CAMBRIDGE • NEW YORK • SHARJAH

Ordering Information
Quantity sales: Special discounts are available on quantity purchases by corporations, associations, and others. For details, contact the publisher at the address below.

Publisher's Cataloging-in-Publication data
Quinlan, Stephen
Icons

ISBN 9798886938838 (Paperback)
ISBN 9798886938845 (ePub e-book)

www.austinmacauley.com/us

First Published 2024
Austin Macauley Publishers LLC
40 Wall Street, 33rd Floor, Suite 3302
New York, NY 10005
USA

mail-usa@austinmacauley.com
+1 (646) 5125767

I am deeply grateful to my family for their unwavering love and support throughout this journey.

I would also like to extend my heartfelt appreciation to Austin Macauley Publishers for believing in my work.

In the 1986 world cup, two of the most iconic moments in soccer history occurred in the same game in Mexico City between Argentina and England. The greatest goal and the most controversial goal. The match was played against the backdrop of the Falklands war between the two countries a few years earlier.

Hand of God

Two moments enshrined,
on Aztec ground,
greatness defined,
and a new King crowned.

'neath blazing sun,
the sleight unseen,
balletic run,
o'er glistening green.

Intervention divine?
or victory stole?
revenge is mine,
and Malvinas' soul.

A tribute to the great Shane Warne who in 1993 produced the most talked about delivery in the history of cricket. This delivery by the leg spinner would change cricket forever and bring back the lost art of leg spin bowling.

Ball of the Century

With cunning wile,
and devious turn,
of forgotten guile,
for cherished urn.

Revolutions made,
defense forlorn,
a vanquished blade,
noblest art reborn.

Kenny Dalglish, known as the King by Liverpool FC supporters not only for his brilliance on the pitch but off the pitch as well.

The King

On hallowed ground,
the best who played,
from Glasgow found,
a King was made.

Worthy of throne,
for the glory and tolls,
he'll never walk alone,
amongst ninety-seven souls.

To the born and bred,
and all who sing,
the King is Red,
long live the King.

Probably the greatest fight of all time, Ali's victory over George Foreman stunned the world.

Rumble in the Jungle

Mocked and riled,
on Kinshasa stage,
his fists reign wild,
in taunted rage.

Off ropes he lies,
for Goliath to slay,
'mid frenzied cries,
of 'boma ye'.

To many people George Best retired too early, a wasted talent. In reality, his career was exactly how it was meant to be. This poem is a cheeky, shrug of the shoulders of a contented genius.

Best

Talent awed,
a conjurer be,
genius flawed,
or spirit free?

Born to beguile,
bright lights' toy,
the maverick style,
of the Belfast boy.

Jonah Lomu was a New Zealand rugby union player who changed the sport forever. Lomu burst onto the scene with a physicality and athleticism never seen before. He sadly passed away aged forty. As a tribute, this poem is written in the style of the Haka, a Maori warrior chant simply stating that while alive he was the greatest and even after his passing was still the greatest.

Lomu

Ka Mate Ka Mate,
a warrior's call,
Ka Mate Ka Mate,
most warrior of all.

Ka Mate Ka Mate,
a warrior's fall,
Ka Mate Ka Mate,
most warrior of all.

One of the most shocking moments in the history of sport. Ayrton Senna lost his life in a high-speed crash at the San Marino Grand Prix in 1994. Ironically, Senna was to wave an Austrian flag at the end of the race as a tribute to Roland Ratzenberger who died in a crash a day earlier. The flag was found in Senna's cockpit.

Ayrton

From Imola pole,
to Tamburello bend,
a tortured soul's,
most violent end.

Sao Paulo sorrowed,
accolades hurled,
a tribute borrowed,
found still furled.

Steven Gerrard cemented his place as a Liverpool FC legend when scoring one of the most important goals in the club's history against Olympiakos in the Champions league. The poem ends with the now iconic commentary.

Olympiakos

A pure strike soars,
through baying cries,
tumultuous roars,
fill Anfield skies.

Kop legend won,
their hero befit,
"What a hit son,"
"What a hit."

In a famous incident during a rugby union match between Ireland and England in Dublin in 1985, the Irish captain Ciaran Fitzgerald was pictured rallying his team with the words, 'where's your f***ing pride?' No audio of the moment exists.

Class of '85

Consigned to fate,
bereft of mind,
the plaudits await,
of moral kind.

O'er nations roar,
'neath Saxon tide,
the battered and sore,
asked, "Where's your pride?"

In the build up to his trilogy fight against Deontay Wilder, Tyson Fury's daughter was born amid serious complications. This poem is about a Fury's toughest fight, not in a ring but in the intensive care unit.

Fury

Toughest fight,
all hope gone,
divine light,
on a gypsy shone.

Gods will,
and the new,
eyes fill,
champion of the ICU.

Manchester United FC was decimated by the Munich air disaster yet incredibly won the European Cup ten years later.

Munich

Flight 609,
…15.04,
etched in minds,
forever more.

From snowy grave,
and burning plane,
the Busby babe,
would rise again.

Probably the biggest scandal in the history of Sport. Lance Armstrong finally admitted to using performance enhancing drugs.

Bloods, Threats, and Gears

Vaunted, jeered,
no fire no smoke,
conscience cleared,
by charity's cloak.

Meteoric rise,
spectacular fall,
yellow prize,
stripped of them all.

Tiger Woods dominated the sport of golf for many years. His sheer presence in his black and red was often his greatest weapon.

Tiger

Aura famed,
born to win,
peers tamed,
in battle's din.

Never before,
seen or said,
Tiger's roar,
in Sunday red.

Ninety-seven people died as a result of the Hillborough disaster in 1989.

The 97

A day to behold,
Wembley again?
But horror unfolds,
on Leppings Lane.

To the pride and joys,
who'll never walk alone,
to the girls and boys,
who never came home.

A fight that was meant to settle the score once and for all still left a sour taste for many as the memory of the insults and slurs never quite went away.

Thrilla

From opening bell,
to settle score,
two step into hell,
to fight once more.

Fists pound and pound,
in titanic duel,
one man crowned,
one blind on his stool.

Dubbed the Thrilla,
every ounce gave,
but taunt of gorilla,
taken to grave.

The shooting star that was Mike Tyson.

Tyson

Misunderstood?
D'amato's wing,
from Brownsville hood,
to rule the ring.

Kill or be killed,
belts unified,
unfulfilled?
No mother's pride.

Mayhem, madness,
addicted, clean,
tragedy, sadness,
the best we've seen.

In Wimbledon's men's final in 2009, Roger Federer was attempting to beat Pete Sampras's record of Grand Slam Titles. Not only that but three legends of the game, Laver, Borg and Sampras himself were there to watch, increasing the tension.

King of Kings

Tension high,
for Kings to play,
history nigh,
on judgement day.

Epic ensues,
on royal green,
three Kings muse,
the best there's been.

Gold in hands,
adulation rings,
alone he stands,
King of Kings.

A tribute to the greatest batsman ever, West Indian Brian
Lara.

The Prince

Flashing blade,
rivals slain,
mere mortals made,
with cold disdain.

Arrogant air?
flamboyant reign,
as Prince of flair,
and Port of Spain.

Paul McGrath was an Irish professional footballer. This poem refers to his struggles with racism, alcoholism and adulation and his relationship with Jack Charlton.

The Black Stuff

Abandoned child,
troubled boy,
youth wild,
bigot's joy.

Demon's clutch,
by bedside stood,
a father's touch,
forgive him, he would.

Legend cast,
in Irish lore,
the chequered past,
Black Pearl
of Inchicore.

Jurgen Klopp became manager of Liverpool FC. He would go on to lead them to the Premier League title after a thirty-year wait.

Messiah

Unto them bestowed,
the new adored,
wind of change blowed,
belief restored.

Return just,
top table to dine,
doubt turned to trust,
like water to wine.

Guiding hand,
ends tortuous trail,
to the Promised Land,
and the Holy Grail.

Barry McGuigan was an Irish professional boxer nick
named the Clones Cyclone whose career coincided with the
troubles in Northern Ireland in the eighties. McGuigan had
the ability to bring together people from both sides of the
divide. Possibly his greatest achievement.

Unified

Tri colors, bands,
red, white, and blue,
'cross troubled lands,
a Cyclone blew.

A people born,
'to unholy divide,
a people torn,
Unified.

Described as the dirtiest race in history, the 1988 100m Olympic final was won by Ben Johnson who was later stripped of his gold medal for drug abuse. Of the eight competitors, only Calvin Smith never failed a drugs test during his career. A real day of shame.

979

For Olympic gold,
and fastest seen,
souls long sold,
by the great unclean.

Beneath the flame,
a dash to the line,
Seoul's day of shame,
in nine seven nine.

Probably the greatest footballer ever, Leo Messi was once described as a gift from God. The title of this poem is inspired by John Keats Ode on a Grecian Urn.

Ode to the Catalan Urn

Art his trade,
canvas our soul,
beauty made,
pure and whole.

If beauty be true,
and we adore,
so Camp Nou,
be Heaven's door.

Romanian gymnast Nadia Comaneci won multiple gold medals at the 1976 and 1980 Olympic games becoming the first gymnast to be awarded a perfect score of 10.0. Despite this, she desperately wanted to be free from her country's communist regime and defected in 1989. This poem is about winning the ultimate prize, freedom.

Ten

At one with beam,
gold galore,
pawn of regime,
craved something more.

Bars perfected,
hands still bound,
bars defected,
freedom found.

Michael Jordan is considered the greatest basketball player ever and is probably one of the most iconic athletes in history. To me, the last play in game six of the 1998 playoffs sums up the career and greatness of Jordan. With thirty seconds left on the clock he steals the ball back, makes his way down the court, shrugs off the tackle and with the last throw, not just of the game and the playoffs but of his Chicago Bulls career wins the title for his team for the sixth time in eight seasons and third time in a row.

Air

A steal late,
Thirty to go,
for six in eight,
and three in a row.

As a bull, last play,
dream is to dare,
the perfect way,
for the man called Air.

What Jesse Owens achieved at the 1936 Berlin Olympics is probably the greatest achievement in sport. What was to be a parade of Aryan supremacy was crushed single-handedly by Owens. Amazingly, Owens was acknowledged by Adolf Hitler but did not receive either a telegram or an invitation to the White House from then President Franklin D. Roosevelt.

Owens

Aryan fair,
'36 Berlin,
myth laid bare,
by different skin.

On foreign soil,
Fuhrer's hand,
back home the spoil,
his like still banned.

Tom Brady is the greatest NFL player ever. His ability to cope with extreme pressure and seemingly have more time than any other player allowed him to perform at the highest level in the biggest games. This is probably what separates him from all other quarterbacks. To date, Brady has an incredible record of seven super bowl rings with New England having six Lombardi trophies and Tampa Bay one.

Lord of the Rings

When mortals fold,
behind the grill,
ice cold,
time stands still.

Lombardi haul,
greatness brings,
and Fame's Hall,
for Lord of the Rings.

Alex 'Hurricane' Higgins was the wild man of snooker in the seventies and eighties and is credited with bringing the game to a wider audience contributing to its peak popularity at that time. A heavy drinker smoker and drug user, Higgins went from being World Champion to being penniless, once mistaken for a tramp. Despite this, he still remained 'The Peoples Champion'.

Hurricane

Wild eyed,
drug fueled,
collars wide,
green baize ruled.

The Peoples Champ,
a tainted reign,
from 'King to Tramp',
The Hurricane.

The 33rd Ryder Cup became known as the Battle of Brookline. The behavior of both the U.S. spectators and U.S. team was criticized by large sections of the media both in America and in Europe. With Europe taking a huge lead into the final day, Ben Crenshaw famously declared he had a good feeling about this. Justin Leonard's putt on seventeen sparked scenes that will never be forgotten.

Battle of Brookline

Head to head,
for the 33rd,
as visitors led,
prophetic word.

Birdie putt,
penultimate green,
forty-five foot,
stampede obscene.

Arguably the most Iconic image in the history of sport, two American athletes bowed their heads, raised their fists and wore black socks and no shoes as a protest at a medal ceremony at the 1968 Olympics. The image is simply bursting with meaning and emotion as there is so much going on in that moment. This poem tries to capture as much of that meaning with every line.

Home of the Brave

Old Glory flies,
heads fall,
Spangled Banner dies,
fists tall.

For the poor, no shoes,
beads, the hanged,
amidst the boos,
America panged.